Kaxla

Forest Animals

Written by DEBORAH HODGE
Illustrated by PAT STEPHENS

Kids Can Press

For Dave, who introduced me to the wonder and beauty
of our Canadian forests — D.H.

For Caitlin — P.S.

I would like to gratefully acknowledge the expert review of the manuscript and art by Dr. Laura R. Prugh, Ecologist and Postdoctoral Researcher, Environmental Science, Policy and Management, at the University of California, Berkeley.

Sincere thanks to my talented editors, Sheila Barry and Lisa Tedesco, for their continued support and hard work. A special thank you to illustrator Pat Stephens for her beautiful art.

Kids Can Press acknowledges the financial support of the Government of Ontario, through the Ontario Media Development Corporation's Ontario Book Initiative; the Ontario Arts Council; the Canada Council for the Arts; and the Government of Canada, through the BPIDP, for our publishing activity.

Published in Canada by
Kids Can Press Ltd.
29 Birch Avenue
Toronto, ON M4V 1E2

Published in the U.S. by
Kids Can Press Ltd.
2250 Military Road
Tonawanda, NY 14150

www.kidscanpress.com

Kids Can Press is a CORUS™ Entertainment company

Edited by Lisa Tedesco and Sheila Barry
Designed by Kathleen Gray
Printed and bound in Singapore

The paper used to print this book was produced with elemental chlorine-free pulp harvested from managed sustainable forests.

The hardcover edition of this book is smyth sewn casebound. The paperback edition of this book is limp sewn with a drawn-on cover.

CM 09 0 9 8 7 6 5 4 3 2 1
CM PA 09 0 9 8 7 6 5 4 3 2 1

Library and Archives Canada Cataloguing in Publication
Hodge, Deborah
    Forest animals / written by Deborah Hodge ;
illustrated by Pat Stephens.

(Who lives here?)
ISBN 978-1-55453-070-0 (bound)
ISBN 978-1-55453-071-7 (pbk.)

1. Forest animals—Juvenile literature. I. Stephens, Pat, 1950–
II. Title. III. Series: Hodge, Deborah. Who lives here?

QL112.H625 2009   j591.73   C2008-903706-5

Contents

What Is a Forest?

A forest is a large area of land covered in trees. Many forests are in northern areas, where summers are short and winters are cold. These are called boreal or northern forests.

The forest is full of amazing animals. Their bodies are built for staying warm in cold weather and living among the trees.

Most trees in this forest have cones and pointed leaves. Animals nibble on seeds in the cones.

The forest is home to many birds. Some stay for summer only, but the great grey owl lives here all year. Whooo-ooo-ooo!

Moose feed at lakes and rivers in the northern forest. In summer, they gobble up water plants.

Black Bear

The black bear is a big, powerful animal with long claws and sharp teeth. Black bears can move a heavy log with one paw!

Frisky cubs, the size of puppies, like to play and explore. Their mother teaches them how to find food and stay safe in the forest.

If danger is near, a cub scurries up a tree. Its curved claws grip the bark.

Zzz … This sleeping bear is snug in its winter den. A layer of fat under its fur will serve as food until spring comes.

The bear is hungry by spring. It uses its long tongue and loose lips to gobble up bugs, nuts and berries.

Chickadee

The chickadee is a tiny bird that flits through the forest. Its black feathers absorb heat to keep it warm.

Chick-a-dee-dee-dee. This flock of chickadees is singing. They use songs to tell each other where the food is or if an enemy is near.

Strong feet hold a chickadee upside down. This helps it find seeds, insects and other food.

A sleepy chickadee keeps out the cold by fluffing its feathers and tucking its head under a wing.

A chickadee mother makes her nest in a hole in a tree. She hisses to scare hungry squirrels away from her eggs. Sss!

9

Lynx

The lynx is a shy, wild cat that hides in thick, bushy areas of the forest. Lynxes look like very large pet cats.

Lynxes live alone, except for mothers who have babies. This mother washes the fluffy new kittens with her tongue. Purr, purr ...

Thick gray fur covers a lynx like a warm winter coat. The color helps the lynx hide. In summer, its fur is brown.

Big, furry feet make it easy to travel over the snow. Long back legs help the lynx jump high and far.

The lynx is a silent hunter. Like a cat stalking a mouse, it watches and waits for a snowshoe hare — then pounces!

Wood Frog

The wood frog stays on the forest floor for most of the year. It catches bugs with its long, sticky tongue.

Skin the color of dead leaves helps the frog hide from hungry birds and snakes. The frog's skin turns darker in the cold.

In winter, wood frogs sleep under leaves or logs. Their bodies freeze like ice cubes! The frogs warm up and wake up in spring.

Croak, croak, croak! That's the sound of wood frogs in early spring. They're saying it's time to hop to a pond and lay eggs.

This tadpole, or baby frog, hatched from an egg. Soon it will grow legs and leap away into the forest.

Woodland Caribou

The woodland caribou wanders in thick forests, with big trees, where it can easily hide from hungry wolves.

In winter, groups of hungry caribou feed on mossy plants, called lichens. Long legs and large hooves help them travel in deep snow.

This caribou is digging for lichens. Its big, sharp hoof cuts into the snow like an ice-cream scoop.

Mmm ... A thick layer of fur is as warm as a woolly blanket. Fur covers most of the caribou's body — even its nose!

A baby caribou can stand a few minutes after it is born. An hour later, the frisky calf can run!

Wolverine

The fierce wolverine has a short, stocky body, like a bear. Wolverines prowl alone in far-off parts of the forest.

A wolverine roams a long way, searching for food that wolves have left behind. It marks its trail with a strong, skunky scent. Phew!

A wolverine's jaws are strong enough to crush bones and chew up frozen meat. Crunch!

A wolverine buries some food for later. Its long, curved claws dig into the snow.

Baby wolverines cuddle in a cozy snow den. Their fur will get thick and brown as they grow.

Loon

The loon's lonely cry echoes over lakes in the northern forest. Loons build a nest and lay eggs here each spring.

Baby loons can swim as soon as they hatch, but they hitch a ride to warm up or rest. Both parents feed and protect the fuzzy chicks.

A loon dives deep into the lake to catch a fish with its long, pointy beak. Gulp!

Splish, splash! Big, webbed feet work like paddles to make the loon a powerful swimmer.

The loon flies to a warmer place for winter. It takes off like a plane on a runway. Zoom!

Snowshoe Hare

The snowshoe hare can run as fast as a car on a city street. It can jump as far as two tall men lying end to end.

Whoosh! This hare is racing away from a hungry lynx. Hares stay safer by looking for food at dusk or dawn, when the light is dim.

Big wide feet work like snowshoes to keep the hare on top of the snow.

A young hare stays very still when enemies are near. Its white fur matches the snow and makes it hard to see. Shh ...

In summer, the hare's fur turns brown. This helps it hide in bushy areas as it nibbles on grasses and leaves.

Wolf

The wolf is a fast runner and powerful hunter. An adult is about the size of a big German shepherd dog.

Wolves live and hunt in a family group called a pack. The pack members protect one another and help care for the playful pups.

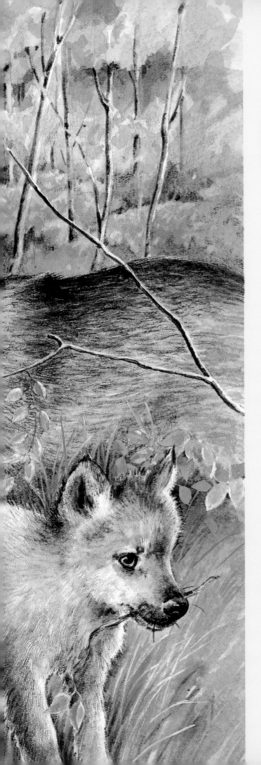

Ruh, ruh, rooooooo! Wolves in a pack "talk" to each other by howling. The sound also tells other packs to stay away.

A wolf has sharp teeth and strong jaws for hunting its prey — the moose and caribou it eats.

Long, slender legs help the wolf run fast and far as it chases its prey through the forest.

Animal Words

Every forest animal has special body parts that help it get food and stay warm and safe. Can you find pictures of these body parts in the book?

beak
page 19

nose
page 15

feet
page 21

claws
page 17

lips
page 7

teeth
page 23

For Parents and Teachers

Boreal forests are found in a circumpolar ring around the northern part of the world and include regions in North America, Europe and Asia. Most trees in the boreal forest are evergreen conifers. A vast system of wetlands, including rivers, lakes, swamps and bogs, runs through the forest, where winters are long and cold. A diverse range of species, adapted to these harsh conditions, makes their home here. All of the animals in this book are found in North America. The lynx, loon, wolverine and wolf also live in Europe and Asia.

Boreal forests are important ecosystems that are affected by human activities such as logging, mining, and oil and gas exploration. Conservationists are working hard to protect the forests and their species. Even so, some species, such as the woodland caribou, are at risk due to habitat loss.